MW00884145

# Virtual Grandma

# Virtual Grandma

A how-to guide on "virtually connecting" with little ones up to age five using FaceTime, Skype, and other apps. For grandparents, aunts, uncles, godparents, overseas military parents, traveling parents, and friends!

**Alison Hillhouse**

Copyright © 2017 Alison Hillhouse
All rights reserved.

ISBN-13: 9781541173354
ISBN-10: 154117335X

# Contents

*To Charlie's grandparents, Mimi, Papa, Gaga, and Big Daddy. May he inherit Gaga's random creativity, Big Daddy's goofiness, Mimi's attentiveness, and Papa's eye for how things work. We are blessed that he could enter this world with four living grandparents.*

# Introduction

You have a little one in your life whom you absolutely adore, whether it's a grandchild, nephew, niece, godchild, a good friend's child, or your own child. You cherish the time you spend together and are always looking to create special memories that build the bond between you two.

But one thing gets in the way—distance.

Your little one may live a six-hour drive away, a six-hour plane ride across the country, or maybe even six time zones away. Or you may be a parent who travels frequently for your job. The distance can be heart-wrenching at times, but you do whatever you can to stay close in spite of it. Often, that involves technology—a cell phone, computer, or iPad. As much as we curse the addictive nature of technology, the fact that it allows us to keep in touch with loved ones is a blessing.

We live just outside of New York City with our three-year-old son, Charlie. His Gaga and Big Daddy live in Missouri, and his Mimi and Papa live in Texas. So using FaceTime (Apple's version of video chat) to connect with his grandparents is a huge part of his life. It's a great way for him to continually build upon the wonderful relationships he's made in person with these special people.

Gaga, a former schoolteacher and creative type, has taken to doing "experiments" to engage Charlie over FaceTime. When I tell other grandparents about these experiments, they are always curious to learn more. They often tell me it's difficult to keep their little one's attention over video chat, that they don't know what to do to spark a conversation. I told one grandmother I met on a playground in Brooklyn about Gaga's "fruit basket" game that she plays with Charlie over video chat. She was intrigued but lamented, "I'm just not that creative to come up with things like that."

Guess what? You don't have to be creative!

We've come up with the ideas for you. This book contains twenty ideas that we have found to be successful in virtually engaging with babies and toddlers. Many of these come from our own creative Gaga, and many have been crowdsourced from other grandparents, aunts, uncles, and godparents across the country.

Each idea is called a "Spark," as it is meant to spark your relationship from far away and help you get to know each other better. Most Sparks involve face-to-face interaction over a video-chat app such as FaceTime or Skype, often with the use of props, such as puppets or fruit. Some Sparks are videos you can create on your mobile phone that your little one can watch over and over again—helping to nurture your relationship even when you aren't face-to-face.

## How to Use This Book
### Think of everything as experimental.

Some Sparks may work great for your little one while some may flop. He or she might love talking about all the fruits in your fruit basket but totally space out on your virtual puppet show. As your relationship with him or her grows, you'll be able to better gauge what kinds of things will and won't work and how to adapt some Sparks so they meet his or her specific needs and interests.

### Keep it low pressure—you aren't a three-ring circus.

It's not easy to consistently engage with children over FaceTime or Skype, given their limited attention span and distractions in their home. Sometimes your little one will be very responsive and want to "talk" for several minutes. Sometimes you might get a laugh and then he or she will move on to playing with his or her trucks. And other times, he or she will just not be in the mood to engage at all (Charlie sometimes tried to switch apps to watch truck videos instead of staying on FaceTime with his grandparents!)

You can't take this personally—kids just want what they want, when they want it. Gaga often finds ways to capture Charlie's attention when he seems distracted, and sometimes she doesn't. It's important to remember that you shouldn't feel pressured to be exciting over FaceTime. The Sparks are merely tools to pull out of your tool kit when you feel up to it.

If you are less theatrical and wish to stick to more basic ideas, Sparks like "Fruit Basket," "Family Mealtime," "Show & Tell," and "Digital Storytime" might be for you. You'll have to just see which ones suit your personality and conversation style. Feel free to dial down (or dial up!) any of the Sparks.

**Use the age guidelines simply as guidelines.**
The Sparks identified in this book are good for babies, toddlers, or preschoolers roughly one to five years old (and even beyond!). But you'll have to assess your little one's developmental pace to determine which ones might or might not work with him or her at each point in time. The Sparks are sectioned off in terms of rough ages when you might want to *first* introduce them. If you are first getting this book and have a toddler, please make sure to go back and read the "Babies" section—all the ideas there will work great for a toddler as well! If you are first getting this book and have a preschooler, please make sure to go back and read *both* the "Babies" and "Toddler" sections—the Sparks will still resonate.

**Experiment with day parts.**

Time of day can make a huge difference in terms of when your little one is willing to virtually engage. One of the grown-ups featured in the book, Uncle Ido, runs scheduling for a TV network. His prime job is to determine which shows the audience will be receptive to at a given time of day (called "dayparting" in the media world). He employs a similar strategy with his niece and nephew in Israel, as he works to figure out what kinds of conversations and interactions work best with them at various times throughout the day.

Toward the end of the day, Ido's niece and nephew are more revved up and will talk about things that happened during the day. But Ido finds the morning chats most special, when they use FaceTime with him from their beds right when they wake up. He says, "They're groggy, and the conversation is more free flowing. They ask me random questions like 'What color is your shirt?' so they can learn the English word for that color. Or they ask to look through my closet or out my window at New York City life. They're less encumbered by the day's events."

**Mix up "live" and "recorded video" ideas.**

Unless otherwise noted, most of the ideas in this book are things you can do live while on video chat with your little one. But we've also provided some "recorded video" ideas, where you create a video for your little one to view over and over in his or her own time (and when Mom needs a "baby-sitter" or distraction). Both are memorable and fun for babies and toddlers and useful for Mom and Dad!

## Gather supplies.

Many of the Sparks require no supplies at all, but some require small investments in things like musical instruments or hand puppets. Supplies that are referenced throughout the book are generally things *you* need at your home (though sometimes supplies are also required at your little one's home). The things described in the book are all very affordable online. Also check out your local dollar store, where you can unearth many treasures to use as part of your conversations and to keep surprising your little one.

## Use any video-chat app.

Throughout this book, we will typically refer to FaceTime, since that is the app that our extended family uses to connect with Charlie on a regular basis. But FaceTime is interchangeable with apps like Skype and Google Hangouts as well as new video-chat apps that appear all the time. Use anything that works for you.

**Be creative with your camera skills.**

Some of the Sparks require you to do something active on your end, which can be a little tricky if you are using FaceTime with a handheld mobile phone. You can invest in an inexpensive bendable tripod to hold your phone for less than fifteen dollars. Prop up your iPad with a case. Try angling your laptop just right to capture what you are doing. Finally, you may need to involve a third person for some of the more involved Sparks, like "Cooking Show."

**Establish an end-of-call ritual, like hugs, kisses, and pressing the red button.**

At the end of a FaceTime call, your little one might be open to giving a virtual hug or kiss to the phone. If he or she isn't, you can take the initiative and blow kisses. While it seems silly, it really is quite sweet. Around age two or three, kids really enjoy being the one to press the red button on the iPhone and end the call.

**Help Mom and Dad out as a "virtual babysitter."**

We all know you can't *really* babysit a child over video chat, but you can entertain an older toddler for ten minutes while Mom or Dad get some much-needed time to wash the dishes or cook dinner. Seriously, FaceTime with Gaga has been a lifesaver when I've needed to send out some work e-mails or just get organized.

## Remember, this book isn't just for grandparents!

It's for uncles, aunts, godparents, overseas military parents, and anyone who wants to connect with a baby or toddler in his or her life. Throughout the book, grandparent/grandchild interactions may be cited a bit more frequently as most ideas have been sourced from grandparents, but all of these ideas can work for any adult and a little one in his or her life.

If you are a Mom or Dad, you can use this book to orchestrate creative interactions between your little one and loved ones in your lives. It means so much to grandparents to have their favorite little faces pop up in their lives. As Nancy of Annapolis says, "When you don't live close to your grandkids and you ache because you miss them so much, it's wonderful to see their little faces on FaceTime. Sometimes, when kisses are given, they accidentally hang up on us...so sweet!"

Also, as a parent, consider how you can help older relatives through difficult or lonely times. Many parents have told us how they've used FaceTime to have their children bring cheer to grandparents in the hospital.

# The Sparks

# CHAPTER 1
## Babies (and Beyond)

We'll start with a few ideas for babies that are incredibly simple and largely intuitive, though hopefully some of the specific examples will spark new ways for you to approach your interactions. Remember, you can't expect much from a baby on the other end, but just seeing your face on a regular basis is an important start to your virtual relationship and building a personal connection. Next time you see him or her, it won't feel as if you've been apart for so long, as you've been virtually building your relationship every week!

Please remember, these Sparks aren't *just* for babies. They can be introduced as early as birth, but should have appeal for toddlers and even preschoolers as well.

# 1. YOUR SPECIAL SONG

*Supplies: None*
*First introduced: At birth*

Special songs that grown-ups sing with their little ones become lifetime memories. Many adults can recall songs and rhymes that their grandparents sang with them as little children.

—∞—

**Choose a song or rhyme to sing to your little one frequently over FaceTime. The song could be an old classic like "Itsy Bitsy Spider" or "Five Little Monkeys," a camp favorite like "Little Bunny Foo Foo" (which has hand motions), a rhyme like "Wee Willie Winkie," or you could even make up your own silly song.**

—∞—

Grandma Linda from Boca Raton created a special song to sing to her granddaughter, Leni, in Brooklyn so that she'd always know it was her, whether she popped into Leni's world on FaceTime or in person. Grandma Linda started singing this song to Leni as soon as she was born. It was simple to come up with and easy for her very little one to understand: *"Hello, Leni (last name). How are you? How are you? Hello, Leni. How are you today?"*

The key here is repetition. Whatever songs you choose, sing them over and over again so your little one begins to associate interactions with you and these special songs. As your little one approaches toddler age, you might want to mix in some new tunes. Hand motions are a big plus—songs like "Itsy Bitsy Spider" and "Little Bunny Foo Foo" have fun hand motions that will increase engagement. A Google search will reveal a bunch of classic songs that you might have forgotten you knew.

Also, as your little one gets older, you can seek out special songs that pertain to her interests. A search on YouTube for "kids' truck tunes" will give you a great variety of songs about bulldozers, dump trucks, and cement mixers. Turn on the theme song to her favorite cartoon and try to sing along.

If you aren't afraid to act really silly, get some colorful scarves and dance around with them. Babies love to watch colorful scarves flow through the air. Many baby-music classes use sheer scarves that adults drape over the heads of their little ones so they see the world in different colors. You can drape a sheer colored scarf over the FaceTime camera to replicate that experience.

Music truly is one of the easiest ways to connect with a little one in person and over FaceTime. If you don't mind singing to a baby who won't respond at all, feel free to start this at birth! Grandma Linda sang Leni's special song as soon as she was born. Even though babies might not respond, they are absorbing your voice. Once your little one is about six months old, he or she will likely show some recognition of what you are doing at the other end!

## 2. MUSICAL-INSTRUMENT LESSONS

*Supplies: Inexpensive instrument(s) for you. Ideally provide the same instrument(s) for your little one at his home.*
*First introduced: Six months*

You might have great talent on an instrument, or simply enough talent to toot out "Three Blind Mice" on a recorder. Whatever your musical ability might be, it is more than sufficient to entertain a baby or toddler over FaceTime.

---

**Whether you're performing your favorite childhood song, a Motown oldie, or a Christmas tune, your little one will love to see you shake your maracas and dance a bit! Turn on your tunes and break out the simple drum or plastic maracas you found online.**

---

Grandma Gigi from Richmond is known in her family for breaking out her maracas and shimmying around at family celebrations. So naturally she started playing maracas to baby Riely as early as six months. Gigi's maracas always accompanied her favorite songs, like "Feliz Navidad," "I Can't Help Myself," and "The Sound of Sunshine." Gigi would sing and get up and dance crazily while an enraptured Riely watched. Eventually, as Riely got a bit older, Gigi gave her a special gift: her own set of maracas to play with Gigi over FaceTime. They now have their own special songs that will make Riely think of her Gigi throughout her entire life.

If you've got a dusty piano in your living room, now's the time to learn to hunt and peck a song or two. Your spouse could film you playing and singing along. You couldn't have an easier audience!

## 3. FAMILY MEAL TIME

*Supplies: Food (sometimes you can arrange for the same food to be on your little one's plate)*
*First introduced: Nine months*

Mealtime is a perfect time to connect—when your little one is confined to one space, is busy eating, and can focus on talking to you over the iPad. You'll find this to be true for babies, toddlers, and even school-age children.

—————

**For this Spark, all you need to do is coordinate with your little one's mealtime. You can be eating too, or virtually eating the same food as your little one. Consider having a regularly scheduled gathering, like Sunday dinner, Saturday brunch, or daily breakfast.**

—————

For our family, breakfast with grandparents has become a morning ritual every few days. What's the main topic of conversation with a baby? What foods everyone is eating! We talk about eggs, fruit, and bread, and try to generate a little enthusiasm around the vegetables that are lying untouched. It can be fun when similar items are on the menu in both homes, so everyone is eating the same thing. For breakfast, the coordination isn't too difficult—fruit, cereal, and eggs are often on the menu in New York for Charlie and in St. Louis for his Big Daddy.

Mom and Dad can show their little one how to virtually "feed" a hungry grandparent over FaceTime. Charlie loves to put his fork up to the computer screen with food on it that his grandparents will pretend to loudly snarf down. They get their mouths up close to screen and "eat" whatever comes through all the way from New York. This activity has long-term appeal—we were surprised to find that it hasn't grown old yet even as he's three years old.

Mimi from California is a regular Sunday night dinner guest at her grandkids' home in New York. Mom Gemma of Long Island says, "Once dinner is ready on Sundays, we call Mimi and she 'sits' at the head of the table and takes part in dinner conversation." Everyone, including Mimi, really feels like part of the meal! Mimi asks questions about what's going on, and the kids recap their favorite parts of the week.

Mealtime works particularly well for relatives in Europe. Mom Jaime from Virginia organizes regular Sunday meals with her kids and their cousins who live in England (of course while it's lunch in the United States, it's dinnertime in London!). She notes that it's "nice to feel like you are all at a table eating a meal together."

# CHAPTER 2

## Toddlers (Ages One to Two, and Beyond)

As your little one grows into a toddler, his or her capacity for more complicated interactions over FaceTime grows. No longer will she just stare at you and occasionally smile, but she will actually begin to engage with you. Your little one will start showing more interest in toys and stuffed animals, which can be integrated into conversations. You can develop shared rituals and jokes that will begin to extend into your real-life time together.

Don't forget, while these Sparks can be introduced to toddlers, *all* of them work for preschoolers as well!

## 4. FRUIT BASKET

*Supplies: At least one piece of fruit*
*First introduced: Age one*

Fruits are typically among the first foods that babies learn to recognize and talk about. Many a child's first word is "'nana." So what better way to connect over FaceTime or Skype than by starting a conversation around your little one's favorite fruit?

---

**To play Fruit Basket, all you need to do is take some fruit and start talking. Ask your little one what you are holding. Peel it, take a bite, talk about its color and taste. If you can, coordinate it so that your little one has the same fruit at his house, so you can experience it together.**

---

Fruit Basket was the very first game that Gaga played with Charlie over FaceTime, so we are especially fond of it. Charlie was just learning to say the names of fruits and ask for "'nanas" and "apps" at home. To his surprise, one day Gaga showed up on FaceTime with a 'nana! He couldn't believe his eyes. He even tried to reach through the screen to grab it!

We peeled bananas and ate them together for days. After that got old, we expanded our fruit palate. We started with fruits that Charlie knew about, like apples and grapes, and then journeyed into fruits he wasn't so familiar with, like kiwis. Some of his first fruit experiences were over FaceTime with his Gaga and Big Daddy. Fruit Basket is another game that can be played well into the toddler years. There are so many fruits that many adults haven't even tried, like starfruit, kumquats, and lychees.

Fruit Basket can be elaborated on as your little one gets older, to help expand his palate to foods beyond fruits. You can help his mom get him interested in eating any kind of new food, especially vegetables. Creative names can help take the bitter bite out of vegetables, like "little trees" for broccoli or "smiles" for slices of yellow pepper.

## 5. UNBOXING (LIVE OR RECORDED VIDEO)

*Supplies: A new toy*
*First introduced: Age one and a half*

This Spark capitalizes on the "unboxing" trend that's swept YouTube. Believe it or not, people have made millions of dollars unwrapping toys and playing with them in YouTube videos, and these are popular with kids around the world. Typically, you only see the unboxer's hands playing with the toy and don't even know the person's identity. Well, it's easy for you to be an unboxer too (though we can't promise you'll get rich!).

—— ❦ ——

**You will need a new toy to unbox. Film yourself slowly unwrapping the toy from the box, playing with it, and narrating minute details about the toy as well as how you are playing with it.**

—— ❦ ——

We often tell Charlie that Gaga sits at home and plays with trucks all day—trash trucks, bulldozers, and dump trucks. His eyes grow wide as he contemplates how similar they are and how exciting her life must be! And there are videos to prove it, short clips we watch repeatedly on the iPhone featuring Gaga playing with toy trash trucks on her kitchen countertop and narrating what she's doing.

The video doesn't need to be long, and you don't need to say anything interesting at all! For example, Gaga got a miniature trash truck that she pushed back and forth on the countertop while she explained what she was doing. The exact narration is as follows: "This is a trash truck! Look how it works. You put the trash in here, open it up, and squash it down. There it goes. It's a good truck!" (Charlie watched this seemingly mundane video over and over and over again.)

And to make it even more exciting, next time you see your little one, actually give him the trash truck to keep!

Charlie was also mesmerized by a video of a car-carrier toy that loaded and unloaded cars over and over again. Each different color car was given a name that he would recite as it entered and exited the car carrier.

It's also fun to unbox Easter eggs filled with little trinkets or candies. You'll find a number of these popular videos on YouTube, but they don't have the special bonus of your voiceover to accompany them.

## 6. STORYTIME (LIVE OR RECORDED VIDEO)

*Supplies: Children's book or recordable storybook*
*First introduced: Age one and a half (more successful as kids get older)*

Storytime is one of the best opportunities to connect with a child who is starting to discover the joy of books. And there is no reason you have to be there in person to read one of your little one's favorite books to him or her. There are many ways to virtually read a book to your little one, whether it's a book that you own, a book you borrowed from the library, or a digital book that you can access with an iPad app. Storytime is a great opportunity for a mom away on business to check in with her family and "tuck in the kids," as she can read a favorite book she's slipped into her suitcase. Alternatively, a made-up story involving her travels can also be fun!

**Buy some favorite books, or dig up your old ones.**
Perhaps the most basic way to start is to simply read a physical book over FaceTime. Search for books that are popular with toddlers today, or dig up books you've saved from your (or your children's) childhood. Be sure to hold up the book so your little one can easily see the pictures. And consider ways to make it interactive—if you are reading *Brown Bear,*

*Brown Bear* to a toddler, try to get her to say the color of the animal, identify what kind of animal it is, or imitate the sound it makes.

Uncle Ido from New York purchased books to read over FaceTime to his niece and nephew in Israel at their bedtime, while he enjoys his afternoon coffee. Two Israeli favorites they like to read are *The Lion Who Likes Strawberries* and *An Apartment to Rent*.

*The Book with No Pictures* by B. J. Novak is also a favorite book for a playful toddler. The book forces the adult reader to say words like "blork" and "blurff," as well as proclaim that your "head is made of blueberry pizza," all of which is immensely funny to a three-year-old. Since the book doesn't have pictures, it doesn't require you to hold it up to the camera. This could be something you start during an in-person visit so that your little one gets the idea of the book, and then you can read it to him virtually in the future.

**Check out the local library.**

"Grandma" of St. Louis goes to her local library to check out books that her grandkids in Colorado will like, and then reads them over FaceTime. Books she's selected include *If You Give a Mouse a Cookie*, *Fancy Nancy*, and *Ladybug Girl*. Dad Rob of Colorado says, "My parents have been reading books to my kids since they were old enough to sit up. They love this time with their grandparents!" He also notes that he is entertained as Grandma struggles through the Spanish words in the *Dora the Explorer* series.

## Go digital.

Perhaps the simplest solution to sharing a book is to use an app, so you can both see the pictures! Apps like Storytime by Kindoma allow you to virtually read classics like *The Three Little Pigs*, *The Tale of Peter Rabbit*, and *Twas the Night Before Christmas* to your little one. The website Readeo (readeo.com) gives you access to more than 150 of the best children's books and allows you to "bookchat," as they call it, with your little one. One of our favorites, *The Circus Ship*, is in their collection of titles. Not only will your little one see the book and be able to virtually turn the pages, but he or she will also see your face in the corner as you read the book. Please note, apps come and go quickly—if these apps are no longer in existence, search "video chat story-time" on Google or in the app store and see what's currently available.

## Try a recordable storybook.

It's not hard to find a book with a built-in voice recorder so you can record yourself reading a book to your little one.

Hallmark has a collection of these, and they are available on Amazon or at local book shops.

Charlie's Big Daddy came across *Goldilocks and the Three Bears* at Dollar Tree and recorded it using a different voice for each of the three bears (he also renamed them "Big Daddy bear," "Gaga bear," and "wee-little-Charlie bear"). Sam, a mom from New York City, noted that Papa Steve read a Disney recordable book to his granddaughter Leni, and his exaggerated Minnie Mouse voice was a huge hit.

**Record a video of you reading a story.**
The great thing about videos is that little ones can watch them anytime, even when grandparents aren't available to chat. Recorded books are a great alternative to TV when Mom or Dad needs a few minutes of peace!

Aunt B from New York City video-recorded herself reading *The Twits* for her niece and nephew in Ohio, in which she prominently featured the pictures to accompany her voiceover. To make a video, record yourself on a computer webcam or iPhone holding the book to face the camera (you might need an assistant to help you prop up the phone). Afterward, you can send the video file by e-mail, or if it is too big, use Dropbox, Google Drive, or another file-sharing service. There's also the option to send it by mail on a flash drive.

New websites make this process much less cumbersome. The site, A Story Before Bed (astorybeforebed.com), guides you in creating a video featuring one of several hundred classic stories. The video will show the pictures in the storybook and a small picture-on-picture video of you reading the book in one corner. The video can then be easily downloaded by your little one's mom or dad.

**Try reverse storytime.**

As your little one learns to read, or at least becomes more adept at making up stories, he or she can take the lead in telling a story to you. An excellent book for little ones who can't read but have an imagination is *Journey* by Aaron Becker. This book has no words but tells a magical story of a girl who travels through an imaginary world with the help of her crayons. Your little one and you can take turns telling different versions of the story.

**Invite guests.**

On both sides of storytime, "guests" can be invited to hear the story. These could be favorite stuffed animals or dolls, but also toy bulldozers that like a good story. You may even have some guests join in on your side—toys you keep for when your little one visits or dolls from your youth. Make a production out of saying hello to your guests and thanking them for coming to storytime.

**Create your own story.**

Sometimes the best stories are the ones you make up or that your little one makes up! Five-year-old Frank from New York and his Pop Pop in Australia play a storytelling game called "Five Words." They collectively decide on five random words that they will each need to incorporate into a creative story. They separately work on their stories over a week, and then next week's call is the "reveal." Even though they use the same five words, the resulting stories are vastly different! One of their favorites was "The Tale of the Tap-Dancing Caterpillar," not surprisingly based on a selection of words including "tap-dancing" and "caterpillar."

If your little one is too young to come up with his or her own story, he might be able to just pick five words or five pictures from a magazine for you to craft your story around. Mom or Dad could e-mail the five pictures to you so that when you're telling the story, you can hold up the corresponding photos. The story could be about animals, construction vehicles, or "PAW Patrol" characters. After a few times, your little one will eventually start drawing the connection that he's helping shape the story.

**Read an ongoing story.**

As your little one progresses to chapter books, consider reading a chapter each night over FaceTime. This is particularly useful for a parent who travels frequently—you can take the book with you and keep the story going, even when you aren't there.

## 7. THESE ARE A FEW OF YOUR FAVORITE THINGS (RECORDED VIDEO)

*Supplies: None*

*First introduced: Age one and a half*

Is your grandchild obsessed with cars? Elephants? Dolls? As I've alluded to, Charlie is obsessed with trucks, especially trash trucks. And he was surprised to discover that trash trucks come to his relatives' homes in St. Louis and Chicago, just like they do for us here in New York.

---

**So get out your phone and film whatever interests your little one! You should narrate it—a simple "Grammy is watching an elephant at the zoo" will do, or "Aunt Sarah is looking at the baby dolls at the toy store. Look at this one in the pink dress!" Just make sure to identify yourself so your little one knows that it was sent by you!**

---

For example, when Gaga heard the beep-beep of the trash truck in her driveway in the morning, she raced out to get a video of the truck pulling in. The first video featured the driver getting out and putting the trash in the truck, the trash being squished, and the truck driving away. It was really blurry, kind of unwatchable, but not to a toddler! Charlie watched it over and over again. The next time, Gaga got the driver to talk on the video. And then she filmed the truck driving up and down the street, which helped Charlie get visual cues to where Gaga lived. It also gave us an opportunity to talk about his grandparents' house and cars in the driveway.

Uncle Doug is also a big fan of truck videos. Anytime he comes across an especially active construction site near his home in Chicago, he stops and films it for Charlie with a narration such as, "Hi Charlie, it's Uncle Doug. Look at that backhoe dump dirt into the trash truck! Did you see that?" Charlie now associates Uncle Doug with all of his favorite things, like bulldozers, forklifts, and cranes.

It doesn't have to be about trucks, by any means. Go to the zoo and track down the elephants. Pop by the fire station and see if one of the firefighters is willing to talk on video. Head to the local American Girl store and have conversations with the dolls. Big Daddy and Gaga have even gone to their neighborhood playground, which Charlie is familiar with, and filmed Big Daddy pushing empty swings, saying, "Next time you're here, I'll push you in this swing!"

## 8. HOUSE TOUR

*Supplies: None*

*First introduced: Age one and a half*

Once your little one has visited your house a few times, he will begin to establish memories of certain things and may even have some favorite things, like the toys you keep for him, a backyard hammock, or your car.

---

**When you are on FaceTime with your little one, take a walk around the house and show him the highlights, from the kitchen to the bedroom where he stays to the car in the garage. Narrate as you go, and zoom in on objects in each room from toys to the fruit basket to framed photos of family members.**

---

Start with the toy box, and remind him of all the toys that are waiting for him next time he comes to visit. For instance, Gaga brings Charlie to "Toy Town," a table she set up in the basement with her collection of cars and trucks. She might act out an impromptu conversation between a few of the cars. Charlie's Papa has also driven around a toy fire truck that is at his house.

Take him to see other things he might enjoy in the house, like the piano in the living room. Gaga usually plays a quick verse of "The Wheels on the Bus" at this stop. Stop at framed photos of little one and even his parent as a child—you'll be surprised how many three-year-olds can recognize childhood pictures of Mom or Dad!

Any novelty item is a good stop on a tour—Aunt Abby has a Goldfish machine in her office, and two-year-old Jonah loves to see her turn the knob so Goldfish spill out into her hand.

Bring him outside. Let him see your backyard, and remind him of things he did there, like swing in the hammock or rake leaves. And don't forget to check out the garage—open car doors, check out the interior, and even honk the horn. The car inspection can be especially exciting for budding car fanatics.

Most importantly, take him on a trip to the bedroom he stays in when he visits. Show him the bed where he sleeps and remind him that it's waiting for him, with a special blanket or stuffed animal. Gaga decorated an entire bedroom with a *Cars* movie theme, complete with a Lightning McQueen chair, a lamp, and a special picture on the wall where the cars all light up. Charlie was first introduced to his special room over FaceTime, and when he arrived at Gaga's house, he couldn't believe it was real!

Nana from Virginia regularly brings her grandson, Caleb, of Brooklyn, on virtual house tours. Mom Lindsey explains, "The main event is the toy room, where Nana plays with Caleb's favorite toys while he watches and plays along. His favorite toy is the barn, so she picks up each animal while he makes the appropriate animal sound. One of the highlights of the house tour is when Caleb calls out for Nana's dog,

Toby, to come over to the iPad! Each session ends with him saying good-bye to the toys, good-bye to the living room, good-bye to "Nana car," good-bye to Toby, and good-bye to Nana! And of course, Caleb has to be the one to press the red button to end the call—but only when he's ready!"

A twist to House Tours might be to have your little one take you around *his* house. Mom Denise of New Jersey notes that when her husband was out of town, her two-year-old son Casey pushed "Dad" (meaning Dad on iPad) around in his toy stroller to show him that everything in the house was still intact!

## 9. PUPPET SHOW (LIVE OR RECORDED VIDEO)

*Supplies: Puppets, Fisher Price Little People, stuffed animals, dolls, or figurines of any kind*
*First introduced: Age one and a half*

For creative FaceTimers, puppets are a unique way to engage feisty little ones on the other end of the call.

———

**Get creative with some inexpensive puppets, Little People, or other figurines next time you talk to your little one! Give them names, personalities, hobbies, likes, and dislikes. And have them act out simple scenarios that might be relevant to your child's life, like trying new foods or going to school.**

———

Oliver, a two-year-old in Brooklyn, is thrilled when a crew of Little People show up in his FaceTime conversations with his Nona of Idaho Falls. One of the Little People has been given the name Oliver, and the others are named after his friends and babysitters. The real Oliver takes an active role in the skits that his grandparents act out with the toy Oliver and his friends. Oliver's mom Kira explains, "He tells the characters what they should do—eat, sleep, take a walk—and my parents act it out. It's kind of like a group puppet show."

Gaga is often accompanied by three puppets when she FaceTimes with Charlie, each with a distinct personality. Monkey is very sweet and affectionate, Raccoon is sneaky, and Bear is a grump. Bear is often busy playing Gaga's piano, where he fluctuates between playing pleasant "fairy notes" on the higher octaves and banging out very angry lower notes when he's feeling moody. Raccoon is often sneaky, eating food from the trash can. Toddlers love to indulge their sense of mischief and see "sneaky" behavior in these storylines!

The puppets act out simple storylines and we talk about what they are doing each day. Often it is something relevant to Charlie's life, like going to school, learning the ABCs, or eating vegetables.

Sometimes during FaceTime, Gaga will "hear" a puppet calling out to her from another room, and we track it down to find out who is anxious to talk to Charlie that day. The puppets travel to New York in Gaga's suitcase, too, and it's always a fun surprise to see which one "decides" to make the trip.

Again, little ones love to see stuffed animals or puppets that are naughty! Kate from England notes that her grandchildren love "Hospital Teddy"—a bear given to her grandson when he was in hospital that now lives with the grandparents. She says, "Sometimes when we FaceTime, Hospital Teddy is waiting center stage to interact with the boys, and we are nowhere to be seen. He stands on his head, peeks round the side of the screen, and throws things about, to the delight of the boys! He makes rude noises and generally does the opposite of what he is told to do."

## 10. BAD COFFEE

*Supplies: A coffee cup*
*First introduced: Age one and a half*

There's not much to this silly game, but it's a hit every time and can be replicated across various food and drinking experiences.

---

**Simply pick up a coffee cup, pretend to drink from it, and then, after a dramatic pause, have an extreme reaction to how the coffee tastes—delicious or disgusting!**

---

Gaga always has a dramatic reaction. Sometimes she'll pro-claim that the coffee is "delicious," and other times she'll scrunch up her face in disgust and say, "Bleeeghh" or "Eww, gross!" Every time, it should be a mystery how the coffee tastes. Even sequential sips from the same cup could have surprisingly different outcomes.

Charlie finds this game hysterical. Gaga will drink "cof-fee" on her end and have a surprising reaction, and some-times she has a reaction to the food that Charlie "feeds" her over FaceTime. This is repeated when Gaga visits and Charlie is taking a bath, when she dips a cup into the water and pretends to drink coffee from it. Charlie has caught on to this and mimics the "bad coffee" reaction in the bathtub (unfortunately, his pretend skills aren't perfect, and he often ends up drinking dirty bathwater).

This is another very simple Spark that will last longer than you think—preschoolers still find the game hysterical.

## 11. SNAIL MAIL

*Supplies: Cards, letters, stickers, coloring books*
*First introduced: Age one and a half*

With all this talk about digitally connecting, it's important to remember that snail mail is still an exciting option. In this day and age, it can feel like a bigger novelty than FaceTime!

※

**Keep a collection of random things to send to your little one—photos of trucks from magazines, cheap cards from your dollar store, sheets of stickers, coloring books to rip pages out of, and more!**

※

Charlie loves getting cards from his Mimi and Gaga. They both do a great job of finding cards that feature images that appeal to him, like fire engines, "PAW Patrol" dogs, Elmo, jack-o-lanterns, and more! He loves pop-up cards and opens and closes them over and over again. In a Halloween card, Mimi popped in a sheet of festive stickers. Gaga sent pages of a "PAW Patrol" coloring book one by one over a series of several mailings, as well as small photos that she and Big Daddy took in a photo booth at a party.

Postcards are a fun idea, especially since you can customize them so easily today. Several mobile apps enable you to create and send them right from your cell phone, so if you capture a fun photo of you or your spouse on vacation, you can send an in-the-moment postcard. Of course, a serendipitous sighting of a bulldozer near your house might be even more exciting for your little one!

## 12. SHOW AND TELL

*Supplies: None on your end*
*First introduced: Age two and a half*

Perhaps one of the most obvious activities to do over FaceTime is to have your little one take you on a tour of his or her room and play with some toys. Children love nothing more than when special grown-ups in their life are just as excited about their toys as they are!

———

**Ask the little one's parent to build excitement for the call, indicating that you are *really* excited to see her collection of dolls or *really* eager to see how she "cooks" in her kitchen.**

———

Mom or Dad might help your little one organize all of his or her dolls in advance to show you or line up race cars for the big virtual race. But show and tell can just as easily be done in an impromptu call. The important thing is that you demonstrate that you are very enthusiastic about seeing his toys. Ask your little one questions about his toys and request demonstrations, such as, "Which of your cars goes the fastest?" "Can you race the police car and the fire truck?" Mom or Dad might need to help position the iPad or computer so you have a clear view of the races. When there's a cooking demonstration, make sure to inquire about all the different foods in the fridge—what is each fruit or vegetable called?

For a slightly older child, dolls could be set up for a tea party, and you could be the virtual guest. Make sure to have a cup of tea and snacks on your end. Start conversation as well. Ask the dolls questions about what kinds of snacks they like, what their favorite colors are, and what they have been up to this week!

## 13. ART GALLERY

*Supplies: Your little one's art, tape, and maybe plastic frames*
*First introduced: Age two*

It seems like kids create an endless amount of art—in school, at after-school classes, and at home. While most art conveniently disappears after a few weeks of being displayed on the fridge, it can also find another home at Grandma and Grandpa's house.

***

**Create a dedicated art gallery of your little one's pictures in your home, and make it a focal point of your virtual conversations. Your little one will feel so proud to have her art "on loan" at a gallery across the country.**

***

The "gallery opening" could be launched as a surprise for your little one. One day you can host a FaceTime tour of your house and announce that you have a new special thing to show her. You then reveal an entire wall of her artwork! The art gallery doesn't have to be located in a high-traffic area in your home. A wall in an unfinished basement, the laundry room, or even the garage would be exciting for a small child. If you have the time, you can back some of the art with colorful construction paper or even find inexpensive frames to make it feel extra special and gallery-like.

Your little one will get excited to ship her art off to your gallery and then see it appear piece by piece. You can talk about your favorite works and which one you look at the most based on your mood. Also, have other family members and friends come by to comment on their favorites. You can then explain, "Today Aunt Sonja came by, and her favorite picture was the sparkly elephant!"

You could also create a nice photo gallery with printed cell-phone pictures of your little one, by stringing twine along a wall and attaching photos with clothespins, a la Pinterest galleries. Your little one will be excited to see which photos Mom or Dad sends you to make the photo gallery, and as you zoom in on newly acquired photos, these can serve as conversation starters, such as "I see that you were playing with your kitchen here. What were you cooking?" For older children, it might be possible to have them play photographer and take their own series of photos for your gallery.

There are several ways this could be orchestrated, but the whole point is to show your little one how big a part of your daily life she is, even if you live far away. You constantly pass by your loved one's art and photos and think about her and what she is doing. And you are always the number-one fan of her work!

## 14. COOKING CLASS

*Supplies: Ingredients for a recipe, at both your home and your little one's*
*First introduced: Age two*

Kids love to cook, even when they are just toddlers! And who better to help them learn some of the basics than you?

—◦◦◦—

**Cooking together requires a bit of coordination. Mom or Dad will need to purchase all the ingredients for the recipe that you are going to teach, and you will on your end as well. Once everyone has all the ingredients, class can begin! It's best to start with one of your little one's favorite foods that have some toddler-friendly steps, like muffins or miniquiches.**

—◦◦◦—

First, talk about all the ingredients that both you and your little one have in front of you for the recipe, and see if he can point them out. Then walk through the recipe step by step, and Mom can help coordinate on the other side. Depending on the child's age, Mom might be doing most of the cooking. But even toddlers can manage some tasks like the following:

- Putting muffin liners in the muffin pan
- Placing puff pastry circles in muffin pans for miniquiches
- Topping miniquiches with cheese, ham, and bacon bits
- Dumping basil into the blender to make pesto
- Rolling out homemade pasta noodles

If you are making something that requires time in the oven, you can call back once the baking time is up. At that point, you and your little one can share a meal or a snack together.

For Charlie's first recipe with his Gaga, she chose a simple Jiffy corn muffin mix and added shredded carrots to get some much-needed vitamin A into our vegetable-rejecting toddler's diet. Gaga and Mom coordinated all the ingredients ahead of time, and Mom preshredded the carrots. Gaga then showed up on FaceTime with a chef's hat on! Charlie loved dumping the ingredients into the bowl, mixing them up, and popping muffin liners into the tin.

As your little one gets older, the recipes can get more complicated and less dependent on Mom and Dad. Grandma can share family heirloom recipes. And an older child can suggest recipes and even look them up on Pinterest. Eventually, it could be fun to try more challenging recipes together or have theme nights based on different cuisines, like French or Mexican.

A great holiday gift would be a small chef's hat and apron for your little one and maybe even some special mixing bowls, spoons, or measuring cups.

## 15. OLD-FASHIONED GAMES

*Supplies: None*

*First introduced: Age two*

It might seem so simple, but it's interesting how few people have thought about translating old-fashioned games into the modern era! Many grown-ups intuitively think of playing Peek-a-Boo with babies over FaceTime, but that's often where it ends.

———∞———

**Rack your brain for some old-fashioned games, and if it's been a long time, there's always Google to help you brush up on the logistics. Think Simon Says, Patty Cake, Hide and Seek, I Spy, Rock Paper Scissors, Ring Around the Rosie—anything you might have enjoyed as a kid!**

———∞———

The rules are really up to you. You can adapt the game based on your little one's age and abilities or consider how to adjust the rules so it works virtually. For a game like Simon Says, you can call out the commands just as you would in person. For Patty Cake, you can both do the hand motions and gently tap the computer screen to clap hands together. Something like Hide and Seek might require a bit more adaptation, with Mom or Dad holding an iPad screen and wandering around the house for you to "find" your little one. Or two-year-old Jonah of New Jersey keeps it simple—he just dumps out the Legos and puts the bin over his head!

I Spy is a simple game for a three-year-old, and the virtual version doesn't require too much adaptation—just double-check to make sure the little one can see what you are "spying" in her screen view of your house. Also, Mom or Dad might need to help focus the camera on what little one is "spying" on her end—toddlers don't have much concept of range of sight over the screen.

Be creative and see how your little one naturally helps you adapt these games. You can also invent games, like "which coffee cup is the sugar packet under?" or "guess how many jelly beans are in this glass."

## 16. PLAY-DOH ARTISTRY

*Supplies: Play-Doh*
*First introduced: Age two*

Children are fascinated by busy hands on screen—hands making things, unwrapping toy boxes, opening Easter eggs, and even squishing and molding Play-Doh. Remember, YouTube can be your biggest source of inspiration for FaceTiming with your little ones! There are an infinite number of "active hands" videos that mesmerize kids. Faceless YouTube stars make thousands of dollars playing with toys onscreen.

—∘∘∘—

**Buy a multicolor playdough pack, and maybe a squisher and some molds. Watch some YouTube videos for inspiration (search term: "Play-Doh") to see "magic hands" making hamburgers, faces with hair, and snakes.**

—∘∘∘—

Now you become the Play-Doh show. It's much easier than you think. You just have to mold the pieces and describe what you are doing as you go along, such as "I'm making a teeny ball. I'm flattening the ball. I'm rolling up the green Play-Doh." You can form letters for your little one to read. Or little people who talk to each other. Or snakes that slither up to the screen.

Once your little one is a bit older, you can teach her how to make things. Search for "Play-Doh hamburger," and you'll find a clever way to make a hamburger using various Play-Doh colors. You can even "cook" homemade playdough together and then decide what to build with it. With older kids, you can both build the same thing and have Mom or Dad vote on their favorite. The possibilities with Play-Doh are truly endless.

# CHAPTER 3

Preschoolers (Ages Three to Five, and Beyond)

As your little one approaches preschool, he or she will be able to take a more active creative role in your virtual conversations. You'll be able to introduce activities that require him or her to be more inventive and directive (asking *you* to do things that entertain him or her). But you'll be surprised—many of the Sparks that worked when he or she was just one-year-old will still be just as entertaining! So begin to introduce new things, but also build on favorite things that you have been doing for a few years that your little one has begun to equate with virtual interactions with you.

## 17. VIRTUAL RESTAURANT

*Supplies: On your end, a specially designed menu. On little one's, a toy kitchen.*
*First introduced: Age three*

We all know how much toddlers love their little kitchens and the accompanying smorgasbord of food tucked inside the fridge and cabinets—from eggs to eggplants to zucchini to broccoli (mind you, much of this food they wouldn't touch in real life). Next time you call your little one, let him know how starved you are for a chef-cooked lunch, and see what delicious meal he can whip up for you with his play foods.

—&#8776;—

**Create a restaurant-like experience at your home. Set the table and place a special menu at your placemat. Invite guests: a stray stuffed animal or your doll from childhood. And then order up some tasty items on the menu for your little one to cook.**

—&#8776;—

Opa from New York likes to dine at a restaurant in Switzerland, where his two grandchildren live. These little Swiss chefs cook him everything from fish to *aubergine* (the French word for eggplant)! Opa has a specially designed menu that he orders from, which features all the food in his little ones' kitchen. He drew pictures of the menu items on the left and wrote the names on the right, so his grandchildren could see the words. Opa explained to his grandchildren that he was able to create a magic hole in the computer screen to receive the food and eat it!

While Opa tends to find all the food delicious, if you have a cheeky little one who likes to be teased, you might not find everything up to your standards. For example, he might make a serious misstep in his fried eggs, and you dramatically spit out this "bad food," scrunch up your face in disgust, and exclaim, "Eww!" Send it back and ask for more!

The menu can be a handmade creation or something you snagged from a local restaurant. If it's handmade, you can even make it with your toddler when you see him in person. Ask your little one what he likes to cook, and write some of these things on the menu. Let him decorate the cover with crayon drawings or food-themed stickers. For an older toddler, establish pricing. (Yes, you might find your favorite baked aubergine costs a hundred dollars.) This is also an opportunity for you to practice counting money with an older child, as you can hold up dollar bills and coins to the screen to "pay," asking him if it's the right amount.

If your little one becomes a big fan of the Virtual Restaurant, continue to add to his or her food and cookware collection. There are so many play-food options these days, from pizza to ice-cream sundaes. And don't forget to give your little chef a chef's hat and apron to wear if he or she enjoys dressing up!

Phew, sounds like a lot of orchestration, right? Don't forget, you can keep this simple and just "eat" the food from your little one's kitchen. You don't need the table setting, the menu, or anything else. But they can be fun additions when you have the energy!

## 18. APP CONNECTIONS

*Supplies: Downloaded apps on your cell phone or iPad*
*First introduced: Age four*

Cell-phone games don't have to be solitary. They are a great way to connect with a far-away little one who is probably already obsessed with her parents' devices.

---

**You might be surprised to know how many apps can help you engage in fun and creative ways with your little one, time zones apart. As mentioned in section six, storytime apps can help you read "virtual books." But that's not where it ends—drawing, face-swap, video-chat, and game apps can also be fun tools for connection.**

---

Pretty much all kids love to play with apps and games on their parents' devices, so why not get in on the fun and create a shared experience? All you have to do is download the same app on both of your devices, and you are ready to go!

Drawtime by Kindoma is an app where children and families can draw together over video calls and messaging. It offers a "shared drawing canvas" for you and the little one to draw on during a live video call. Not only can you draw, but you can play tic-tac-toe or practice letters with your little one. To find more apps like this, search for "video chat draw-ing" in the app store.

Some apps also feature classic games like Memory, Go Fish, and Old Maid. For example, MemoPlay allows you to play Memory while video-chatting with your little one. As noted earlier, apps come and go, but likely with a bit of searching you will find the latest apps that work for you. It can take a bit of research to find games that are good for little kids that you can play along with, but start by search-ing for "video chat kids' games."

Of course there are the usual options that you might already be using yourself, like Snapchat or the Photos stream on your iPhone. On Snapchat, your little one will immensely enjoy sending and receiving selfies overlaid with silly filters. And she could have a special "Photos" stream on Mom or Dad's iPhone where she and Grandma can upload silly pho-tos of themselves in their day-to-day lives or on trips. Make sure to comment on her photos to show how much you are enjoying them!

## 19. PRACTICE MAKES PERFECT

*Supplies: None*
*First introduced: Age four*

Whether your little one is practicing an instrument, learning to spell words, or doing speech-therapy exercises, you can serve as the perfect audience, coach, or cheerleader for his efforts, even when you are thousands of miles away. While Mom and Dad might be busy getting dinner on the table after a long day of work, you might have more patience and energy to sit and provide some virtual support for your loved little one.

─◦◦◦─

**Depending on the practice, have Mom or Dad equip you with what you need to be a virtual coach—for example, a list of this week's spelling words or specific instructions on how you can help your little one with his speech-therapy exercises.**

─◦◦◦─

For a toddler, a great place to start is the ABCs. Have your little one simply practice reciting the ABCs, or you can hold up letters written on notecards and quiz him. Ask what words start with the letters you are showing. You can make or buy cheap flashcards with pictures on them, asking your little one to identify what's on the flashcard and what letter it starts with. There are animal flashcards, truck flashcards, and even princess flashcards available on Amazon.

If you have a budding performer, you could send special dance costumes or other dress-up clothes, and your little one can perform live over FaceTime. He or she could perform gymnastics or a dance show, or a little one clad in a firefighter's outfit could practice extinguishing fires from Lego buildings. For any kind of performance, you can be the most appreciative and complimentary of audiences!

This Spark can extend well beyond the preschool years. Monique, a mom in Brooklyn, actively engages Grandma Diane from Pittsburgh in "practice time" for her seven-year-old daughter. She texts a picture of her daughter's weekly spelling word list to Grandma Diane so that she can help her practice the words for Friday's spelling list over FaceTime. Grandma also serves as an audience for violin practice every few weeks. As Monique says, "It's a way to switch up practice and make it more fun. It allows Grandma to see her grand-child play the instrument, gets us ready for recitals, and changes the dynamic in a positive way."

## 20. LIVE WATERCOLOR PAINTING

*Supplies: A watercolor book of his favorite cartoon characters*
*First introduced: Age three*

Back in the 1980s, the oil-painting phenom Bob Ross was hugely popular on his TV show *The Joy of Painting*. With his soft voice and gentle demeanor, he mesmerized viewers who watched him paint landscapes and "happy little trees" on PBS. America found him to be calming and meditative, and now you can be the painter, offering a bit of prenap, calming respite in your toddler's busy life.

———

**Purchase a cheap watercolor book of your little one's favorite cartoon characters and a set of paints. Set up your art station and paint the characters while you describe what's happening in the scene.**

———

Charlie loves Blaze and the Monster Trucks and enjoys watching grown-ups paint his favorite trucks more than actually painting them himself. He likes to dictate the colors of each car while we paint them for him. As a three-year-old, it's tricky for him to stay in the lines, but he seems to enjoy how an adult can precisely paint the colors into the different shapes on the page.

A watercolor book isn't essential—you can freehand draw things with crayons or paints as well. However, for many little ones, the integration of their favorite characters from TV and the plot lines offered in the books might make it just a bit more appealing. You can also use a coloring book and crayons in lieu of watercolors.

The setup can be a little tricky and might require a small bendable tripod, or perhaps you could angle your laptop just right to capture what you are painting.

You could also try to have identical coloring books on each end and paint at the same time, discussing how your pictures are the same or different.

## Go forth and spark conversation!

I hope you've found inspiration for future virtual interactions that not only seem like they'd appeal to your little one but also suit your personality. It's just as important that your virtual interactions are fun for you, too! While your little one can at times be challenging to captivate, he or she is still the least judgmental audience you will ever have to perform for.

Experiment, make mistakes, act goofy, and just see what works! There are no rules to being a virtual grandma—or grandpa, uncle, aunt, or traveling parent. You are a pioneer—part of the first generation to forge a new kind of relationship with the littlest generation of digital natives.

### Thank you!

Thank you to all of the grandparents, parents, uncles, aunts, and friends who have contributed such creative ideas for this book! By sharing your stories, you will help others build connections with their little ones all across the world. You are digital pioneers, helping foster a new kind of relationship in a new world!

Abby, Ami, Aunt B, Carrie, Denise, Doug, Gemma, Gilmer "Gigi," "Grandma," Grandma Diane, Grandma Linda, Kate, Kira, Heidi, Ido, Jaime, Jane, Kate, Lindsey, Meg, Mimi,

Monique, Nancy "Nana", Nicole, Nona, Opa, Papa Steve, Pop Pop, Rob, Samantha, and Sarah.

...and Charlie's grandparents, John "Big Daddy," Nancy "Gaga," Mike "Papa" and Vickie "Mimi."

Thank you to Eminence System for the illustrations! (www.eminencesystem.com).

**Storytime video-chat apps available in the iPhone app store (as of January 2017)**

Caribu: Caribu.co
Readeo: Readeo.com
A Story Before Bed: astorybeforebed.com
Storytime from Kindoma: Kindoma.com
MemoPlay

Made in the USA
Monee, IL
21 December 2019

19337437R00049